**This book is to be returned on or before
the last date stamped below.**

Customs Around the World

# FOOD
## Around the World

by Wil Mara

raintree

a Capstone company — publishers for children

Raintree is an imprint of Capstone Global Library Limited, a company incorporated in England and Wales having its registered office at 264 Banbury Road, Oxford, OX2 7DY – Registered company number: 6695582

www.raintree.co.uk
myorders@raintree.co.uk

Edited by Gena Chester
Designed by Julie Peters
Original illustrations © Capstone Global Library Limited 2021
Picture research by Jo Miller
Production by Spencer Rosio
Originated by Capstone Global Library Ltd
Printed and bound in India

978 1 3982 0258 0 (hardback)
978 1 3982 0257 3 (paperback)

British Library Cataloguing in Publication Data
A full catalogue record for this book is available from the British Library.

Acknowledgements
We would like to thank the following for permission to reproduce photographs: iStockphoto: FotografiaBasica, 11, kali9, 10, RuslanDashinsky, 15; Shutterstock: AHPhotosWPG, 8, BarthFotografie, 13, Dado Photos, 20, Dragon Images, 28, IuliiaIR, 22, Karpenkov Denis, 24-25, Marc Sitkin, 17, Marc Sitkin, 19, Masson, 6, Monkey Business Images, 1, Odua Images, 5, Primestock Photography, 21, Rawpixel.com, 4, Robyn Mackenzie, 23, rontav, 27, Sergey Ryzhov, 7, Subbotina Anna, Cover, Timolina, 14, vm2002, 9, wantanddo, 16. Design elements: Capstone; Shutterstock: Stawek (map), VLADGRIN

# CONTENTS

Words in **bold** are in the glossary.

# WONDERFUL FOOD

What do you like to eat? Food is important. It gives us energy to work and play. But food can also be fun. We enjoy how it tastes and smells. We share a meal with family and friends.

People around the world have many food **customs**. This means groups have their own ways of eating. They have favourite foods. Food says a lot about people. It can be as special as a person's home, clothing and language!

# MORNING MEALS

What do you eat in the morning? It depends on your **culture**. Culture is how a group lives life. Some eat small breakfasts. Many adults drink coffee or tea. In Greece, a person might have bread with cheese and olives.

**Morning food in Greece is simple.**

porridge

Children in many places eat cereal
for breakfast. It can be cold. Or it can
be hot. In Iceland, some children have
porridge. A little sugar makes it sweet.

Are you feeling extra hungry? In other cultures, breakfast is bigger. Some people in Canada like eating bacon and sausage. Waffles and pancakes fill their plates too. They top it all off with sticky maple **syrup**.

**Many Canadians use maple syrup in their breakfasts.**

**Youtiao with soya milk**

A popular morning food in China is *youtiao*. It's a stick of fried **dough**. It's light and crunchy. People dip it into soya milk. The milk is sweet. Yum!

# FOOD DURING THE DAY

People are often busy during the day. Some eat food that is easy to take to school or work.

Sandwiches are eaten for lunch around the world. Many are made with meat and salad. Some children in the United States like theirs with peanut butter and jam.

**Making peanut butter and jam sandwiches**

empanadas

People in Argentina may grab an empanada. It is bread shaped in a semicircle. It's easy to hold. Inside is a tasty filling. Ground meat is a favourite.

In some cultures, lunch is a big meal. People take a longer time to eat.

Lunch in France can have three parts called **courses**. School lunches are the same. Children eat a salad first. Next is the main course. A famous French dish is quiche. This creamy flan is made with eggs and milk. Cheese, meat and vegetables may be mixed in.

To finish their meal, children have cheese and fruit.

A slice of quiche

# DINNER TIME

Dinner is the biggest meal in some cultures. It is in the evening. Do you eat dinner with your family?

Families in Russia often start dinner with a bowl of soup. They have many **recipes**.

A Russian soup made with beetroot

Injera is eaten by hand.

People in Ethiopia eat a big spongy flatbread called *injera*. Thick **stews** are spooned on top. More bread is put on the side. Everyone tears off a piece with their hands. They use the bread to scoop up the stew.

**Spices** are important when people in India make dinner. In some homes, they create their own mix of spices. It's added to rice, **lentils** and vegetables. Some people in India eat meat too. Others don't. No matter what, the spices make the food special.

A person in India sells spices that will later be used in cooking.

**Tortillas with other food on top**

Many meals in Mexico include tortillas. These flatbreads are used in lots of ways. They can be folded to hold other food. They are then fried, baked or eaten plain.

# SNACKS AND SWEETS

Are you feeling hungry between meals? Then grab a snack! In South Africa, people enjoy biltong. It's a salty meat snack. The meat is dried out for a few days. Then it is cut into thin slices ready to eat.

In Thailand, people sometimes munch on fried insects. Small stalls sell them on the street. The insects are crunchy and crispy.

Stalls in Thailand sell fried insects as a snack.

Do you like sweet food? People in Brazil eat dessert after most meals. One treat is *brigadeiro*. This chocolatey ball is rolled in sprinkles. It's thick and gooey.

brigadeiros

**puff-puffs**

In other cultures, people don't usually eat sweets after meals. But they may enjoy a treat during the day. In Nigeria, people eat puff-puffs. They are fried dough balls. A bit of sugar can be put on top to make them sweeter.

# CELEBRATION FOOD

Holidays are special times. Do you eat any foods to **celebrate**?

A Christmas favourite in Romania is cabbage rolls. The recipe is hundreds of years old. The rolls are stuffed full of meat and rice. Then they are cooked for hours in tomato sauce.

Cabbage rolls are cooked together in one pot.

Making mince pies is a Christmas custom in the UK. Many years ago, they were filled with ground meat and dried fruit. Today, the small pies are made with fruit and sweet spices.

donuts

Some holiday foods have special meaning. The food reminds people of something important.

Jewish people celebrate the holiday Hanukkah. Many in Israel and other places eat potato pancakes called *latkes*. They also have jam doughnuts. These foods are fried in oil.

latkes

The oil reminds Jewish people of a Hanukkah story. According to the story, long ago, a small bit of oil burned for eight days. Using oil in cooking honours that story.

Muslim adults **fast** during the holiday month called Ramadan. They don't eat from sunrise to sunset. Everyone celebrates when the fasting is over.

Many people look forward to eating sweets. A favourite in Pakistan is *sheer khurma*. This pudding is made with milk and toasted noodles. In Lebanon, they make biscuits called *ma'amoul*. Inside is a sticky filling of dates and nuts.

Ma'amoul are a fun holiday treat.

Food brings people together. In many cultures, people learn the recipes their parents make. Others create new dishes. But everyone gathers around when the food is ready. What will you eat next?

# MAP

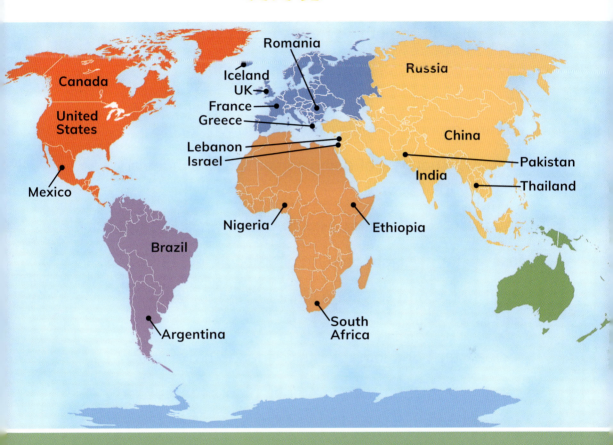

Romania
Iceland
UK
France
Greece
Lebanon
Israel
Canada
United
States
Mexico
Russia
China
Pakistan
India
Thailand
Brazil
Nigeria
Ethiopia
Argentina
South
Africa

Around the world, people eat different foods. See which places were talked about in this book!

# GLOSSARY

**celebrate** do something for a special event

**course** one part of a meal that is brought out on its own

**culture** group of people's beliefs and way of life

**custom** usual way of doing something in a place or for a group of people

**dough** mix of flour and a liquid, such as milk or water

**fast** go for a certain amount of time without eating

**lentil** flat, round seed of a plant related to beans and peas

**recipe** steps and ingredients needed to make a dish

**spice** ingredient made from dried plants that is used in cooking to add a special taste

**stew** dish that is thicker than soup and is cooked for a while

**syrup** sweet and sticky liquid made from sap inside trees that is often added onto other food

# FIND OUT MORE

## BOOKS

*Food (The Science Behind)*, Casey Rand (Raintree, 2012)

*Food Like Mine: Includes Amazing Recipes from Around the World*, DK (DK Children, 2017)

*The World's Strangest Foods (Library of Weird)*, Alicia Z. Klepeis (Raintree, 2016)

## WEBSITES

**www.bbc.co.uk/newsround/48634709**
Learn about some foods that children eat around the world.

**www.dkfindout.com/uk/space/life-in-space/food-in-space**
Find out about food in space!

# INDEX